GETTING TOGETHER

GETTING TOGETHER

Icebreakers and Group Energizers

Lorraine L. Ukens

An Imprint of Jossey-Bass Inc., Publisher

Published by
Pfeiffer, an imprint of Jossey-Bass Inc., Publishers
350 Sansome Street
San Francisco, California 94104
United States of America

Editorial Offices:
(415) 433-1740, FAX (415) 956-3158

Orders:
USA (800) 274-4434
FAX (800) 605-2665

Contents

Group Energizers

*Additional participants may be accommodated. See individual Activity Note.

Introduction

Groups, large and small, are drawn together in a variety of situations that lead to some initial anxiety or expectancy common with new experiences. Group facilitators can get things started off on the right foot by employing some warm-up activities, often referred to as "icebreakers." These activities help support the early stages of the group's development or energize the group for work.

An icebreaker event is an organized activity used to acquaint the members of a group with one another, to form them into partnerships or teams, or to promote openness and sharing. Before beginning a topical presentation, it is important to help team members get to know one another and build a sense of comfort as well as a sense of belonging.

The activities in this book have been divided into two categories: **Icebreakers** and **Group Energizers.** Although all the activities can be considered icebreakers, the main objective of the **Icebreaker** category is to have participants become acquainted and mix together, while **Group Energizers** help invigorate the group and build team cohesion.

Groups can be formed in a variety of ways, but one of the best is when group members are introduced by an activity that serves as a mixer or get-acquainted device. Beginning group involvement in this way provides the facilitator with some control—from the beginning—and promotes interaction among the participants.

Icebreakers and group energizers can help pave the way for the main subject area to follow. Therefore, it is recommended that an activity be chosen that relates to the theme or goal of the upcoming session. The opening activity can be used as an experience from which inferences may be drawn pertaining to the discussion topic. It also provides an opportunity for participants to begin to feel comfortable with sensitive or emotional issues.

Generally, it is better to err on the side of conservative risk taking rather than to have participants left feeling manipulated or vulnerable. This is especially true when the topical issues are sensitive or controversial. In this way, you will be able to lead the group progressively to new levels of skill, trust, and creativity.

Group size also will affect choice of activities. The facilitator needs to match the process to the size of the audience. Suggested discussion areas and procedures are presented for most activities, but you should determine the activity's appropriateness to individual groups. With a smaller group, you may wish to have every individual report. With a larger group, you may need to limit the discussion to the smaller work groups or have one reporter present for each team. Whatever procedure you choose to use, you should allow participants the opportunity to process what has occurred during the activity and to relate it to the session that will follow.

The time estimated for an activity is an approximation and may be adjusted accordingly. Generally, the larger the group, the longer the time required for the activity.

Getting Together: Icebreakers and Group Energizers can help promote appropriate group dynamics and provide participants with an introduction to the subject matter that is to follow in the training session.

Icebreakers

1 ♦ Big To-Do

Objective

To discuss individual role models and their influence.

Group Size

Up to thirty-two participants who will form work groups of four members each. (See note below for ways to accommodate additional participants.)

Time Required

Approximately fifteen to twenty minutes.

Materials

One Big To-Do Card for each participant.

Preparation

Duplicate each page (four pages total) of the Big To-Do Cards on a separate sheet of card stock and cut each page into individual cards. (Each individual page of Big To-Do Cards provides two sets of four cards, for a total of eight participants; four pages provide enough cards for thirty-two participants.)

Note: You can accommodate additional participants by duplicating the Big To-Do Cards in a variety of colors. Players need to match colors as well as the character, the two to-do entries, and the magnet symbol.

Process

1. Distribute one individual Big To-Do Card to each participant.

2. Explain that several famous people arrived earlier and posted their to-do lists with a special magnet, but a mix-up has occurred. It is now the job of the players to form groups that match the name of the famous figure with the two appropriate to-do entries and the corresponding ornamental magnet. Instruct participants to begin searching for their matching players with complementary cards.

3. After the individuals have mingled sufficiently to form groups of four with corresponding cards, instruct members to discuss, one at a time in subgroups, their personal role models and how these figures have influenced them.

Big To-Do Cards

SANTA CLAUS	**FEED REINDEER**
	**LOAD SLEIGH**
BEN FRANKLIN	**FIX KITE TAIL**
	**POLISH KEY**

Big To-Do Cards

SHAKESPEARE	**CALL GLOBE THEATRE**
	**GET NEW QUILL**
ROBINSON CRUSOE	**MEET FRIDAY**
	**COLLECT COCONUTS**

Big To-Do Cards

COLUMBUS	CHECK MAPS
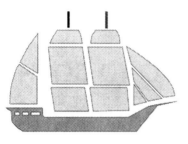	VISIT ISABELLA
SHERLOCK HOLMES	VISIT WATSON
	CLEAN PIPE

Big To-Do Cards

MICHAEL JORDAN	**BUY SNEAKERS**
	**GO TO COURT**
FLORENCE NIGHTINGALE	**ROLL BANDAGES**
	**STARCH CAP**

2 ♦ Box Bingo

Objective

To acquaint participants with one another by playing a game of Bingo.

Group Size

Twenty-five or more participants.

Time Required

Twenty to thirty minutes.

Materials

Index cards, 3" × 5", cut in half (one 3" × 5" card makes cards for two participants); one Box Bingo Worksheet and a pencil for each participant; a box large enough to hold all the cards; prizes (optional).

Process

1. Distribute a blank index card and a pencil to each participant. Ask participants to write their names on the index cards provided.

2. Collect the cards and place them in the box. Cards will be drawn from the box later in the activity.

3. Distribute one copy of the Box Bingo Worksheet to each player. Inform participants that they will locate twenty-four other participants and enter their names on the worksheet, one name per block. The worksheets will be used later to play a game of Bingo. Then tell the participants to begin. Allow sufficient time for participants to circulate together to gather enough names to fill out their Box Bingo Worksheets.

4. When participants have completed this task, announce that the Bingo game will begin. (Participants may want to be seated during the game.) Using the box of names, you will draw out and announce twenty-four participant names, one at a time, and each participant who has the corresponding name on his or her Box Bingo Worksheet should place an "X" over it. The first person(s) to get "Bingo"— all names crossed off the worksheet in a row (either horizontally, vertically, or diagonally)—wins the game. You may give a small prize to the winner(s).

BOX BINGO

		FREE SPACE		

3 ◆ Bullseye

Objective

To encourage sharing and the building of relationships among the participants.

Group Size

Twenty-five participants, who will form work groups of five members each.

Time Required

Approximately fifteen minutes.

Materials

The appropriate number of Bullseye Arrow Puzzles (each puzzle has five separate pieces, and each participant will receive one piece of the puzzle). One set of five Bullseye Arrow Puzzle sheets will accommodate twenty-five participants.

Preparation

Duplicate the Bullseye Arrow Puzzle in five different colors (one color per copy). Cut each puzzle into five separate pieces as indicated by the dashed lines.

Process

1. Distribute one piece of the Bullseye Arrow Puzzle to each participant.

2. Instruct participants to form groups of five members each by locating players with other puzzle pieces that combine to form one complete arrow; each piece of the puzzle must be a different color.

3. When participants have formed subgroups of five members and have completed their puzzles, announce the discussion topic. Instruct the participants to take turns in their subgroups completing the starter phrase, "Something I do well is...."

Bullseye Arrow Puzzle

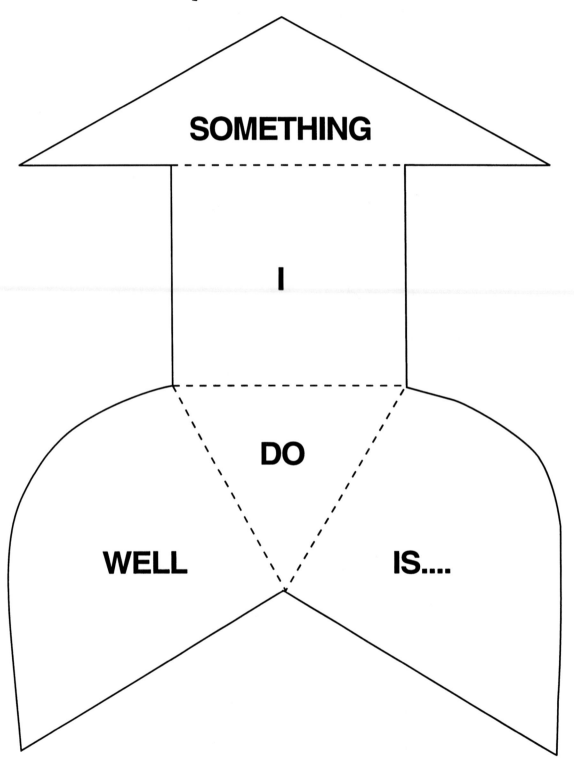

SOMETHING

I

DO

WELL

IS....

4 ◆ Comic Capers

Objective

To encourage groups to share their feelings about organizational issues in a nonthreatening way.

Group Size

Unlimited, but determined by the number of comic strips utilized.

Time Required

Ten to fifteen minutes.

Materials

Assorted comic strip panel sets.

Preparation

Gather a variety of comic strip panels (e.g., Dilbert®). Paste each comic strip panel on card stock and then cut each strip into separate panel pieces.

Note: The number of panels in each comic strip will determine the size of the subgroups formed. Cartoons related to a variety of organizational issues (e.g., communication, teams, creativity, motivation, values, culture) are best suited for discussion purposes.

Process

1. Distribute one cartoon panel piece to each participant. Explain that participants are to locate the other players who have panels that complete their comic strips.

2. Tell the participants to begin.

3. After participants have located their comic strip partners, they are instructed to form the comic strip panels in the appropriate order.

Variation

Several large cartoons may be cut into a specified number of pieces for group members to assemble.

Discussion

Members of the newly formed subgroups can discuss how the cartoon relates to their current organizational culture.

5 ♦ Common Scents

Objective

To acquaint participants with one another by matching scents in a sniffing game.

Group Size

Unlimited. Participants will work with another partner during this activity.

Time Required

Fifteen to twenty minutes.

Materials

Empty film canisters (or similar-type containers with caps)—one for every two participants; a variety of "scents" (e.g., lemon, lime, vanilla, root beer, rubbing alcohol, perfume); cotton balls (one for each scent used); masking tape; a felt-tip marker.

Preparation

Before the session begins, prepare the scent containers. Soak a cotton ball in a different scent and place each cotton ball in an individual canister. Then number each canister on both the bottom and the top using masking tape and a marker (keeping a record of scents and appropriate numbers in case you are asked later to identify a particular scent).

Note: You will need one scent canister for every two participants; each container should have a different scent.

Process

1. Divide the group into two equal teams. Explain that animals have an acute sense of smell, and that parents can distinguish their own offspring from others. For this activity, one team will represent animal "parents" and the other team their "offspring."

2. Distribute one prepared scent canister to each member of the "parent" team. Instruct the parent group members to remove the canister caps and to memorize their particular scents. Next, collect the canisters, letting the parent participants keep their own canister caps.

3. Mix up the canister bottoms and place them on a table. Finally, direct each member of the "offspring" group to choose one canister, but not to reveal the number or the scent selected.

4. Explain that each "parent" must now locate the correct "offspring" by sniffing the canisters to find the matching scent. Have the offspring members stand still, holding their canisters out for the parents to sniff.

5. After all the parents have found their offspring, ask everyone to check their numbers to make sure they match. Partners should look for common personal interests and discuss them with each other.

6 ◆ Defining Moments

Objective

To encourage participants to exchange information about themselves by matching definitions with words.

Group Size

Up to thirty participants, who will form work groups of five members each. (See note below for ways to accommodate additional participants.)

Time Required

Fifteen to twenty minutes.

Materials

Defining Moments Card sets (each participant will receive one card).

Preparation

For thirty participants, duplicate each page (six total) of the Defining Moments Cards on a separate sheet of card stock and cut each sheet into individual card sets. Each page provides one complete set of five cards for a total of five participants.

Note: You can accommodate additional participants by duplicating the Defining Moments Cards in a variety of colors. Players must match color, word, and definitions.

Process

1. Distribute one Defining Moments Card to each participant. Explain that participants are to match their word card with its appropriate definitions by finding other participants with complementary cards (each word has four corresponding definitions).

2. When the various groups have formed, have team members remain in their subgroups and discuss their favorite books, explaining the reasons for their choices.

Variation

Use one-word synonyms rather than more complete definitions for each chosen word.

Defining Moments Cards

PLAY

Literary work
performed
on stage

Occupy oneself
in amusement

Perform on a
musical instrument

Engage in a
sporting game

Defining Moments Cards

DUCK

Aquatic bird with broad flat bill

Durable, heavy cotton material

Lower the head or body to avoid something

Push suddenly under water

Defining Moments Cards

COVER

Protect or conceal something	Travel or pass over a distance
Protect by insurance	Something that is used to shield

Defining Moments Cards

LACE

Draw
and tie
together

Delicate
web-like
fabric

Cord or ribbon
for a shoe
or garment

Streak
an object
with color

Defining Moments Cards

DIRECT

Control
or
manage

Show or
indicate the way
to some place

Conduct
a show or
performance

Straightforward

Defining Moments Cards

DIP

**Plunge
briefly
into water**

**Downward
slope**

**Lower
then raise
in salute**

**Creamy
food
preparation**

7 ◆ Eagle's Nest

Objective

To form discussion groups by constructing a picture puzzle.

Group Size

Unlimited. Participants will form subgroups of four members each.

Time Required

Approximately fifteen minutes.

Materials

Eagle's Nest Puzzles (each complete puzzle, duplicated in a different color, is enough for four participants).

Preparation

Duplicate the two-sided Eagle's Nest Puzzle in a variety of different colors (using the same color for the front and the back of the sheet), choosing the appropriate set of discussion questions for the back (see variation below).

The eagle puzzle appears on side one, the discussion topics appear on side two (there are four discussion topics on side two). Cut each sheet into four separate pieces (one for each discussion topic) as indicated by the dashed lines on the puzzle design. Thus, each two-sided page will provide one complete set of four cards, enough for a total of four participants (four cards, all of the same color, per complete set).

Process

1. Distribute one puzzle piece to each participant. Explain that each player is to locate others with matching color pieces to form a complete puzzle picture.

2. After the work groups have formed, members are to take turns in their subgroups discussing the topic on the back of their individual cards.

Variation

You have been supplied with two different sets of discussion topics for the Eagle's Nest Puzzles. The first set uses discussion questions that are less personally revealing; the second set is recommended for more experienced working groups.

Eagles' Nest Puzzle

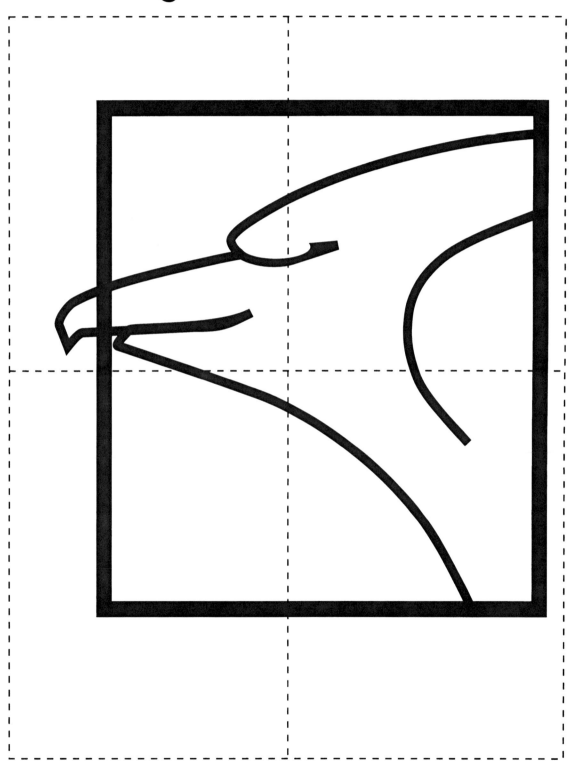

Eagles' Nest Puzzle

Discussion Questions

FAVORITE ANIMAL

FAVORITE FOOD

FAVORITE COLOR

FAVORITE PERFORMER

Eagles' Nest Puzzle

Discussion Questions

PET PEEVE

HERO OR HEROINE

GREATEST ACHIEVEMENT

BIGGEST BLUNDER

8 ♦ Facts of Life

Objective

To determine whether the personal statements made by each participant are true or false.

Group Size

Unlimited. Participants will form work groups of no more than five members each.

Time Required

Fifteen to twenty minutes.

Materials

Blank sheets of paper and pencils (optional), one for each participant.

Process

1. Divide the entire group into work groups of no more than five members each.

2. Instruct participants to take a few minutes to think of three statements about themselves, two statements true and one statement untrue but seemingly conceivable. (*Optional*: You may wish to distribute blank sheets of paper and pencils to participants so that they can write down their statements.)

3. Instruct participants to take turns discussing their three statements within their subgroups.

   As each group member takes a turn, the other members of the group must reach a consensus on which of the three statements is untrue. Groups should be encouraged to discuss why they believe the statements are false.

Variation

Participants tell either a believable lie about themselves *or* reveal an unbelievable truth. It is up to the other group members to decide whether they are hearing fact or fiction.

Discussion

The facilitator leads a discussion about the results of the activity, utilizing the following questions:

- ♦ How well did each group perform on guessing the untruths?

- ♦ Were there a variety of reasons offered to explain why the group reached the same decision?

- ♦ How did your own expectations of an individual influence the decisions?

9 ♦ Frozen Treats

Objective

To share information as participants "freeze" with a partner.

Group Size

Unlimited.

Time Required

Ten to fifteen minutes.

Materials

None.

Process

1. Give participants an overview of the activity's instructions and then instruct them to begin circulating through the room.

2. When the facilitator calls "FREEZE," the participants stop. Then the leader announces "PAIR," and the participants form pairs by turning to the person closest to them.

3. After the pairs have formed, the leader instructs each pair to conduct a discussion on a theme (see suggested topics below). The discussion continues until the leader calls "TIME."

Variation

The process is repeated as many times as desired, with a variety of discussion topics.

Discussion

Suggested themes for discussion topics include:

- ◆ Fun Vacations
- ◆ Favorite Movies
- ◆ Hobbies
- ◆ Sports

10 ♦ Global View

Objective

To encourage discussions of diversity and global influences through the matching of country, landmark, and currency.

Group Size

A maximum of eighteen participants, who will form work groups of three members each. (See note below for ways to accommodate additional participants.)

Time Required

Fifteen to twenty minutes.

Materials

Global View Cards sets.

Preparation

Duplicate each page (three pages total) of the Global View Cards on a separate sheet of card stock and cut into individual card sets. Each page provides two sets of three cards for a total of six participants.

Note: Accommodate additional participants by duplicating the card sets in a variety of colors. Players then match colors as well as country, landmark, and currency.

Process

1. Distribute one Global View Card to each participant. Tell the players that they are being assigned as international goodwill ambassadors.

2. Explain that group members are to locate other participants who have cards to complete their set; a complete set includes the country name, its currency, and a landmark associated with that country.

3. As groups form, players should discuss what each one knows about that particular country.

Discussion

The following questions are suggested for discussion ideas:

♦ How does diversity play a role in today's organizations?

♦ How does the global economy affect the future of business decisions?

Global View Cards

NETHERLANDS	**GREAT BRITAIN**
GUILDER	**POUND**

Global View Cards

FRANCE

ITALY

FRANC

LIRA

Global View Cards

UNITED
STATES

CHINA

DOLLAR

YUAN

11 ◆ Hum-Dingers

Objective

To form discussion groups by locating other participants who are humming the same song.

Group Size

Unlimited.

Time Required

Fifteen to twenty minutes.

Materials

Song cards (3" × 5" index cards, one card for each song selected); a felt-tip marker.

Preparation

Using 3" × 5" index cards and a felt-tip marker, write the name of one familiar nursery song on each card, creating multiple numbers of the same card based on the number of participants. Suggested songs include:

- ◆ "Twinkle, Twinkle Little Star"

- ◆ "Old MacDonald"

- ◆ "Mary Had a Little Lamb"

- ◆ "Row, Row, Row Your Boat"

- ◆ "Three Blind Mice"

- ◆ "Frere Jacques"

Note: You will need to make as many index card copies of each song as the number of subgroup members desired (e.g., if you have eighteen participants and you want them to form into groups of three, create three index cards for each of the six selected nursery songs).

Process

1. Distribute one Hum-Dinger Song card to each participant and request that the information not be shared with others.

2. Explain that each person will hum the melody on the card and will attempt to locate other group members who are humming the same song.

3. Give a signal to begin and allow time for the group members to interact and form discussion groups.

Discussion

After participants have found their respective song groups, you may want to assign a discussion topic. You may choose a topic that is relevant to your current training *or* ask the subgroups to discuss how distractions interfere with the communication process.

12 ◆ The Hunt Is On

Objective

To find other participants who share similar characteristics or preferences.

Group Size

Unlimited. However, the optimum number of participants is restricted by the size of the room. Participants need ample room to mingle with one another.

Time Required

Fifteen to thirty minutes.

Materials

A pencil and one The Hunt Is On Worksheet for each participant.

Process

1. Distribute a pencil and one The Hunt Is On Worksheet to each participant. Direct participants to fill in their personal answers to the questions in the "Self" column.

2. When all group members have completed the "Self" column of the worksheet, instruct them to go on a "people hunt" to find other participants with the same characteristics. As they circulate and locate people who match characteristics, they should have those individuals sign their name in the "Other" column of the worksheet corresponding to the characteristic. Participants should continue asking questions of other participants in an attempt to fill in all the boxes on their worksheets.

3. You may announce a predetermined time limit for the "hunt" or announce a two-minute warning before calling "TIME." (Or the hunt can end when an individual fills in all the boxes on his or her worksheet.)

Discussion

♦ Were you able to complete the sheet?

♦ Which characteristics made it more difficult to find a match?

♦ How can we capitalize on the similarity of individual characteristics or preferences?

♦ How can we utilize differences?

The Hunt Is On

	SELF	OTHER
Favorite Color		
Favorite Ice Cream		
Favorite Sport		
Favorite Hobby		
Favorite Season of the Year		
Favorite TV Show		
Favorite Holiday		
Number of Siblings		
Birth Month		
Eye Color		
Dream Vacation		
Automobile Color		

13 ◆ In This Corner

Objective

To discover common interests and preferences among participants.

Group Size

Unlimited.

Time Required

Fifteen to twenty minutes.

Materials

Visual representations of a selected topic (e.g., pictures that represent each of the four seasons), which should be posted separately in the corners or on different walls of the room.

Preparation

Choose any individual difference dimension as the focus of the activity. Suggestions include:

- ◆ Favorite Season (Fall, Winter, Spring, Summer)

- ◆ Favorite Music (Jazz, Classical, Country, Pop/Rock)

- ◆ Favorite Sport (Baseball, Basketball, Football, Hockey)

- ◆ Type of Animal to Be (Lion, Bear, Giraffe, Fox)

Post the visual representations, one in each corner of the room. Usually there are four separate corners, but three or more corners (or walls) can be used.

Process

1. Direct participants to choose one of the dimensions that represents their own individual preference and to move to the corresponding posted area.

2. After subgroups have formed based on the participants' choices, members within each group should take turns sharing the reasons for their choice.

Variation

After subgroup members have shared their reasons for choosing the same dimension, participants mix with other groups to share the reasons for their choices and to discuss differences in interests/preferences.

Discussion

This activity's structure is designed to allow group members to get to know one another better and to accept one another's choices and preferences. Working with the reassembled group, the facilitator can lead a general discussion on the importance of utilizing a variety of ideas and viewpoints when working in groups.

14 ◆ Limerick Lines

Objective

To create a nonsense verse that requires a creative ending.

Group Size

Unlimited. Participants will form work groups of four members each.

Time Required

Twenty to thirty minutes.

Materials

One Limerick Card and a pencil for each participant.

Preparation

Duplicate each page (two pages total) of the Limerick Cards on a separate sheet of card stock and cut each page into individual card sets. Each page provides two limericks (each limerick is comprised of four cards) for a total of eight participants (each participant receives a card showing one line from a limerick).

Note: Each page of two limericks should be copied onto as many different colored sheets as necessary for the number of participants involved. In other words, if both pages are copied once on blue paper, there are enough limerick lines for sixteen people; if both pages are copied once on both blue *and* yellow paper, there are enough limerick lines for thirty-two people. When the total group is not divisible by four, the people who are "extra" may join another group with the same limerick cards.

Process

1. Introduce the activity by explaining that a limerick is a nonsense verse form which is believed to have come from the city of Limerick in Ireland. Explain the basic rules of a limerick:

   ♦ A limerick has five lines.

   ♦ The first two lines and the last line rhyme.

   ♦ The third and fourth lines rhyme.

   You may wish to provide an example of a limerick (your own or the one given here):

   > *There was a small boy from Carlsbad*
   > *Who wouldn't leave Mom and Dad.*
   >   *Their friends said, "Don't worry,*
   >   *Time goes in a hurry.*
   > *Before long, he'll be a college grad!"*

2. Distribute one Limerick Card to each participant.

3. Instruct participants to keep the limerick rules in mind as they try to locate the other three persons who have matching color cards to complete the first four lines of a limerick. When the four members have formed a group, they are to write a fifth line (which rhymes with lines one and two) to complete the limerick.

4. When all groups have finished writing the fifth line of their limericks, a representative from each subgroup shares the entire limerick with the reassembled large group.

Limerick Cards

There was a young
girl from France

There was a young
lad named Palmer

Who had lessons to
learn how to dance

Whose Mom asked
him to call more

But she stayed
in her seat

He picked up
the phone

Because she had
two left feet

But she wasn't
at home

Limerick Cards

There was a young
man from Toledo

There came an odd
fellow to Willow

With a head shaped
like a torpedo

Carrying a big,
fluffy pillow

He tried on
a wig

He searched
high and low

But his head
was too big

But had nowhere
to go

15 ♦ Many Happy Returns

Objective

To form discussion groups and share information by assembling greeting card jigsaw puzzles.

Group Size

Unlimited. Participants form groups equal to the number of pieces in each puzzle.

Time

Ten to fifteen minutes.

Materials

Greeting card puzzles. (Each participant receives one puzzle piece.)

Preparation

Cut a variety of greeting cards into jigsaw pieces. (Note: The number of pieces into which each card is cut will determine the number of participants for each subgroup formed.)

Process

1. Distribute one puzzle piece to each participant. Direct players to locate other participants with matching pieces to complete a greeting card.

2. When each group forms, members should discuss an assigned question (see discussion below).

Variations

1. Rather than assign a discussion topic, instruct each group to write a four- to six-line verse appropriate to its assembled greeting card.

2. Use young children's jigsaw puzzles that contain large pieces (generally fewer than ten pieces).

3. Use magazine pictures pasted onto card stock, cut into jigsaw pieces.

Discussion

Groups can discuss a question related to the topic of the event or they can discuss a general "get-acquainted" topic, which could include one of the following examples:

- ♦ Family (spouse, children, parents, siblings)

- ♦ Birthdate and place of birth

- ♦ Most memorable birthday celebration

- ♦ Favorite holiday

16 ◆ Moniker Medley

Objective

To acquaint participants with one another by conducting interviews to explore individual names.

Group Size

Unlimited. Participants will work in groups of three members each.

Time Required

Twenty minutes.

Materials

One Moniker Medley Interview Sheet for each work group.

Process

1. Explain that a "moniker" is another word for someone's name or nickname. Some names have a long family history, reflect an important event, or carry some personal significance. (Offer some examples from your own family or from historical figures.)

2. Divide the participants into work groups of three members each, counting off so each member knows the number to which he or she is assigned.

3. Distribute one copy of the Moniker Medley Interview Sheet to each group. Explain that each member will become an interviewer for one other person in the group. (For example, Member #1 asks Member #2 questions; Member #2 questions Member #3; and Member #3 queries Member #1.)

4. Begin by instructing each group's Member #1 to ask Member #2 each question on the Moniker Medley Interview Sheet, asking for further clarification if necessary. When the interview is complete, the interview sheet is passed to Member #2 who will question Member #3 in the same manner. Finally, Member #3 receives the interview sheet and asks the questions of Member #1 to complete the interview process.

Discussion

After all groups have completed the interviewing assignment and have reassembled, ask some volunteers to share the history of their names and/or other responses to some of the interview questions. Discussion questions include:

♦ How does a name influence one's impression of an individual?

♦ How accurate are these perceptions?

♦ What are the results of these perceptions?

Moniker Medley Interview

What is your full name?
(First, Middle, and Last)

Is there an interesting family history associated with your name?

Do you like your name?

Do you know any other people with the same first name as yours?

Do you have a nickname?

What would you like to be called if you could have another name?

What interesting experiences have you had associated with your name?

17 ◆ Name Chain

Objective

To learn the names of the other group members.

Group Size

Unlimited (best when used with large groups). Participants will work in large subgroups (preferably at least five members, but no more than twelve members each).

Time Required

Fifteen to twenty minutes.

Materials

One sponge ball (or a similar soft object) for each work group formed.

Process

1. Instruct participants to form work groups of no more than twelve members each; give a sponge ball (or other soft object) to each group. Instruct each group to form a circle and to give the ball to one of its subgroup members.

2. Subgroups are given instructions for starting the Name Chain. The first person turns to the second person and hands over the ball while saying his or her name. The second person turns to the next individual and hands over the ball while repeating the first name of the preceding person and adding his or her own name. The third person repeats the procedure (repeating the names of all the persons preceding and adding his or her own name), and so on until each person in the circle takes a turn. Thus, the list of names lengthens as the activity continues. The chain is complete when the first person repeats all the names in

the group. If a participant has trouble with the growing list of names, some coaching from the other players is allowed.

3. After this first round in the Name Chain is complete, participants can become more familiar with one another by having one member call out the name of another member while tossing the ball to that person. This process can be repeated for several minutes.

18 ◆ Official Orders

Objective

To become acquainted with other participants by following assigned "official orders."

Group Size

Unlimited.

Time Required

Fifteen to twenty minutes.

Materials

An Official Orders Number Card, an Official Orders Worksheet, and a pencil for each participant.

Preparation

Official Orders Number Cards can be prepared by cutting 3" × 5" index cards in half and writing one number per card until you create enough cards to equal the total number of participants. If name tags are used instead of cards, the numbers may be written directly on them.

Process

1. Each person is assigned a number card (or a name tag), which is to be held (or worn) so that it can be easily seen. Each person is also given a pencil and an Official Orders Worksheet. The worksheet lists assignments that the participants

must do in order, one after the other, by circulating among the other participants and filling in their assigned tasks.

2. When participants find a match, they should record that person's assigned number and first name in the space provided on the worksheet.

3. You may set a predetermined time limit or announce a two-minute warning before calling "TIME." You could also end the activity when an individual fills in all the "orders" on his or her worksheet.

Official Orders

ASSIGNMENT	NO.	NAME
Find two people who own pets.		
Find two odd-numbered players who have blue cars.		
Find one person who has traveled to Europe.		
Find one odd-numbered players with blond hair.		
Find two even-numbered players who wear glasses.		
Find three blue-eyed players.		
Find one even-numbered player who has a birthday in the same month as you.		

19 ♦ The Right Connections

Objective

To encourage cooperation by having participants form a series of word connections created by linking picture symbols.

Group Size

Up to twenty-four participants. (See note below for ways to accommodate additional participants.)

Time Required

Fifteen to twenty minutes.

Materials

One picture from the set of Word Connection Cards for each participant.

Preparation

Duplicate each page (three pages total) of the Word Connection Cards on a separate sheet of card stock and cut into individual card sets along the dashed lines. Each page has eight different pictures. The three pages will be sufficient for a total of twenty-four participants (twenty-four individual cards).

Note: You may duplicate extra cards to accommodate additional participants.

Process

1. Distribute one Word Connection Card picture to each participant. Explain that each card has a picture on it representing a particular word. The object of the game is to form the longest possible line of participants by connecting the last letter of one word to the first letter of another word. (For example: A picture of a ROS<u>E</u> would connect to a picture of an <u>E</u>G<u>G</u>, which would connect to a picture of a <u>G</u>IRAFFE, and so on.)

2. Tell the group to begin forming the word connection line.

3. End the activity by calling "TIME" after approximately ten to fifteen minutes.

Discussion

How willing were other players to adjust their place in line to accommodate a better arrangement?

Word Connection Cards – #1

Word Connection Cards – #2

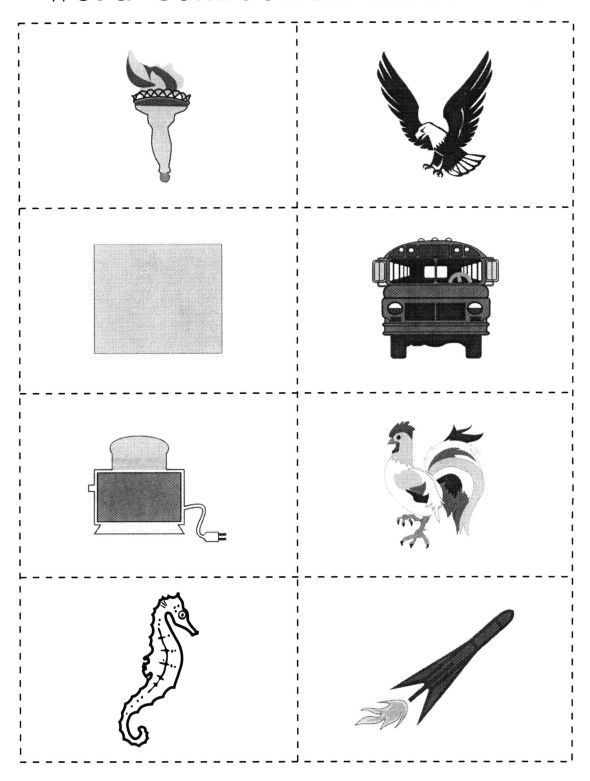

Word Connection Cards – #3

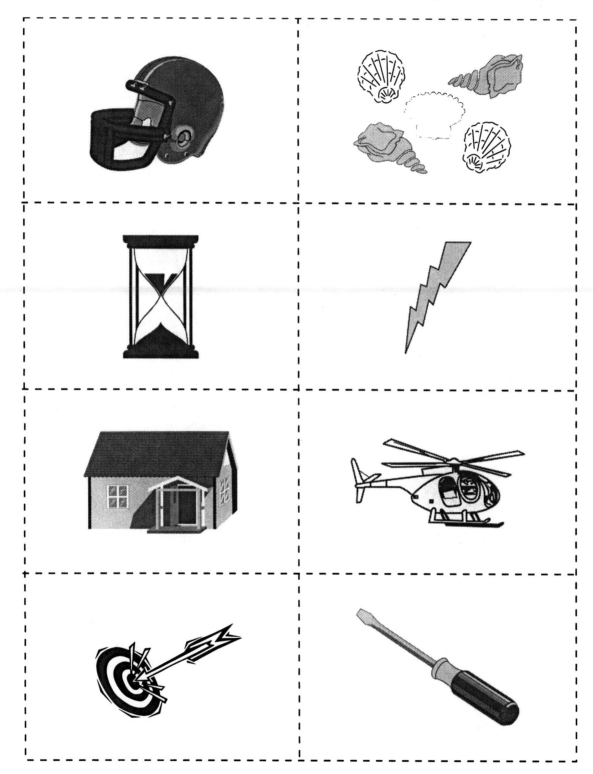

20 ◆ Spelling Bee

Objective

To have participants work together to create word combinations from letters of the alphabet.

Group Size

Unlimited; this icebreaker works especially well with a large group.

Time Required

Twenty to thirty minutes.

Materials

An alphabet card (a 3" × 5" index card with a letter), a Spelling Bee Worksheet, and a pencil for each participant; a felt-tip marker; prizes are optional.

Preparation

Write a letter of the alphabet on each of the 3" × 5" index cards (you will need a card for each participant), using a variety of letters. Use heavy lettering so that the letters are easy to see. It is not necessary to use all twenty-six letters, but a wide variety should be used, particularly vowels (which you may want to use several times depending on the size of the group), so that participants can create words from the letters on the cards.

Process

1. Give each participant a pencil, one alphabet card, and a Spelling Bee Worksheet.

2. Explain that the object of the spelling bee is for participants to gather together into groups with other participants who have letters that form a word. Each time a word is formed, the participants of that group should enter the word on their Spelling Bee Worksheet. After forming one word, the group then separates and the players seek new word combinations with other participants.

3. Start the spelling bee. Allow enough time for participants to form as many word combinations as possible. A prize may be given at the end of the activity to the person having the longest list, or to the members of the group that formed the longest word.

Spelling Bee Worksheet

_____

_____

_____

_____

_____

_____

_____

_____

21 ♦ Talking in Circles

Objective

To encourage communication by having participants move from partner to partner discussing specific topics.

Group Size

Unlimited.

Time Required

Twenty to thirty minutes.

Materials

Chairs (optional).

Process

1. Instruct participants to form two concentric circles with an equal number of members on the inside and the outside. (If there is an uneven number of participants, announce that one group of three is to be formed each time.)

2. After the circles have been formed, announce a topic for discussion (see bulleted discussion items below) and instruct participants to engage in a discussion on that topic with the person facing him or her in the other circle (i.e., one person on the inside circle works with a person on the outside circle).

3. After a few minutes have elapsed, the leader gives a signal for each participant to move to the left a prescribed number of spaces. The leader then announces a new topic, and the two new partners begin a conversation until the facilitator calls "TIME." This procedure may be repeated as often as desired.

Variations

1. This activity may be done to music, as in Musical Chairs. When the music starts, the two circles move in opposite directions until the music stops. Each participant halts and begins a conversation on an announced topic with the person he or she faces in the other circle.

2. Instead of working on an assigned topic of conversation, participants can use the conversation time to find out as much as possible about their partners.

Discussion

Assigned topics can include specific issues related to the organization or group, or a general topic such as the following:

♦ Capital Punishment

♦ Foreign Trade

♦ Space Exploration

♦ Free College Education

♦ Youth Curfews

If a light-hearted approach is preferred, you might choose topics that are less threatening, such as:

♦ Spending $1 Million

♦ Dream Vacation

♦ Alternative Career Choice

22 ◆ What's in a Name

Objective

To assign positive attributes to another person and to discuss how others are evaluated.

Group Size

An unlimited number (divisible by two); participants will work with a partner.

Time Required

Twenty to thirty minutes.

Materials

A pencil and a What's in a Name Worksheet for every participant.

Process

1. Distribute one copy of the What's in a Name Worksheet and a pencil to each participant. Direct each individual to print his or her name vertically in the Letter column on the worksheet, placing one letter on each line as illustrated in the example. If someone's first name is very short (four letters or less), you may wish to have them use their last name instead—*or*, after worksheets are exchanged, the individual's partner can write two responses for each letter of the name (see step 2).

2. Next, instruct participants to form partners and to exchange papers with that partner. Participants are instructed to write a positive adjective or descriptive phrase (based on the letters in each row of the worksheet) describing the other person.

Note: If this activity is used with individuals who are not familiar with each other, point out that the descriptions can be of a general nature, such as physical features. However, if the participants come from intact work groups, encourage them to emphasize aspects of the other person's behavior or personality.

3. When step 2 is complete, the partners exchange the sheets again so that each person has his or her original worksheet. Partners should discuss with each other some of their reasons for providing a particular response. Participants should determine if their initial assessments are "on target."

Discussion

♦ How difficult was it for you to assign the descriptive attributes?

♦ How do outward appearances affect our evaluations of others?

♦ How do our own perspectives play a role in these evaluations?

What's in a Name Worksheet

EXAMPLE

J	jokes with everyone
A	asks opinions of others
C	courteous
K	keeps everyone focused

LETTER	ADJECTIVE OR PHRASE

23 ♦ Who Could It Be?

Objective

To encourage interaction and cooperation by having participants try to identify their assigned characters.

Group Size

Unlimited.

Time Required

Twenty to thirty minutes.

Materials

A Character Identification Sheet for each participant; a felt-tip marker.

Preparation

Make Character Identification Sheets from construction paper, writing the name of a different famous person in large letters on each sheet. (You will need as many Character Identification Sheets as you have participants.) Select real or fictional figures from the past or the present in a variety of fields (e.g., Robin Hood, Abraham Lincoln, Judy Garland, Queen Elizabeth, Houdini, Michael Jackson, Superman). Each sheet of paper should be punched with two holes in the upper corners, and a string consisting of about two feet of yarn should be placed through the holes and tied to the corners in a large loop.

Process

1. Distribute one Character Identification Sheet, face down, to each participant and instruct participants not to turn over their sheets or show them to others. At your signal, each person is to turn to another participant and place his or her sheet around that individual's neck so that the name of the character appears on the player's back (and the character is not revealed to the person wearing the identification sheet). Every participant will give a Character Identification Sheet to another participant and will receive a Character Identification Sheet from another participant.

2. Players move around the room attempting to find out which characters they are. They seek help from other group members by asking up to three questions that can be answered *only* with "Yes," "No," or "I don't know" responses.

3. Once players discover who they are, they turn their sheets around and wear their identities on their chests. Participants should continue to circulate with others, giving hints to those who have not yet discovered who they are.

4. End the activity by calling "TIME" or when all participants have discovered their identities.

Variation

Names of animals can be substituted for famous figures.

Group Energizers

24 ◆ Alphabet Soup

Objective

To give participants practice in collaborating with other team members by combining objects and letters to form defined words.

Group Size

Unlimited. Participants will form work groups with a maximum of five members each.

Time Required

Fifteen minutes.

Materials

A pencil and an Alphabet Soup Worksheet for each participant.

Process

1. Divide participants into work groups of up to five members each. Distribute one copy of the Alphabet Soup Worksheet and a pencil to each participant.

2. Explain that the teams will work together to solve the clues on the worksheet by combining common objects and letters that sound out the words described. For example, the clue "fixed opinion" would translate to "B + leaf" (belief). Announce that the time limit will be ten minutes. (The short lines on the worksheet represent letters; the longer lines represent common objects.)

3. After the designated time is over, get feedback from the teams as you review the solutions.

Solutions

(1) B + tray + L

(2) can + O + P

(3) L + bow

(4) pill + O

(5) chair + E

(6) N + tire + T

(7) A + corn

(8) cat + L

(9) C + saw

(10) E + quill

(11) S + cape

(12) D + feet

(13) X + seed

(14) crow + K

(15) P + can

(16) R + door

(17) fan + C

(18) pen + E

(19) O + mitt

(20) car + S

Discussion

♦ How did the size of the group affect productivity?

♦ How did it affect the quality of the work?

Alphabet Soup Worksheet

(1) disloyalty   _____ + _____

(2) cloth covering   _____ + ____ + ____

(3) arm joint   ____ + _____

(4) "head rest"   _____ + ____

(5) slot machine fruit   _____ + ____

(6) whole   ____ + _____ + _____

(7) oak tree fruit   _____ + ____

(8) steer   _____ + ____

(9) playground equipment   _____ + ____

(10) same as   ____ + _____

(11) run away   ____ + _____

(12) conquer   ____ + _____

(13) beyond the limit   ____ + _____

(14) mallet game   _____ + ____

(15) pie nut   ____ + _____

(16) passion   ____ + _____

(17) highly decorated   _____ + ____

(18) "copper head"   _____ + ____

(19) leave out   ____ + _____

(20) stroke   _____ + ____

25 ◆ Balloon Bounce

Objective

To develop cooperation and team interdependence through using balance and coordination.

Group Size

Unlimited. Participants will form work groups with a maximum of ten members each.

Time Required

Fifteen minutes.

Materials

Inflated balloons (two to three balloons for each subgroup).

Process

1. Divide the participants into work groups of up to ten members. Distribute one inflated balloon to each group.

2. Instruct the members of each group to hold hands in a circle. Explain that the challenge for each group is to bounce the balloon in the air without the players letting go of their hands. If the balloon lands on the ground, the players must pick it up and get it bouncing again without letting go of their hands.

3. When players get better at the balloon bouncing task, give each group another inflated balloon to keep afloat. If time allows, you can give a third balloon to each group to keep in the air.

Discussion

♦ How well did the group work together to keep the balloon(s) in the air?

♦ How do we equate this accomplishment to a team's interdependence?

26 ♦ Closer Observation

Objective

To test participants' ability to remember details and to work together in groups.

Group Size

A maximum of twenty participants, who will work in groups with up to five members each.

Time Required

Twenty to thirty minutes.

Materials

One Closer Observation Worksheet and a pencil for each subgroup; approximately twenty-five to thirty objects of considerable variety (e.g., a button, a pencil, a book, an eraser, toys, etc.); a cloth cover; a table.

Preparation

Prior to the session (and before participants have entered the room), place the objects on top of a table and cover them with a cloth.

Process

1. Divide the participants into work groups of up to five members each. Distribute one Closer Observation Worksheet and a pencil to each group. Tell each group to select one member to act as recorder for the team.

2. Explain that each team will view the objects on the table for a brief period of

time, and then the teams will attempt to describe what they saw using the Closer Observation Worksheet. The more detailed the description of the object, the higher the score. However, points will be subtracted for incorrect answers. Explain that the scoring works as follows:

ADD: 1 point for each **correct object** listed.
1 point for each **correct detail** of an object.

DEDUCT: 2 points for each **incorrect object** listed.
1 point for each **incorrect detail** of an object.

3. Invite all the participants to gather around the table; then remove the cloth that covers the objects. After everyone has studied the objects for one minute, cover them up again. Each team then meets together and compiles a list of the objects that they remember seeing. Allow approximately five minutes for the groups to interact and record their responses on the worksheet.

4. At the end of the allotted time, tell the groups that each recorder should compare the team's list against the descriptions you will provide. Uncover the objects and describe each object in detail, one by one.

5. After you have described all the objects, instruct the team recorders to tally their scores using the scoring system explained earlier. You may need to circulate among the groups and assist in the scoring. For example, if one object on the table was the 8 of diamonds playing card, the scoring would be calculated as follows:

playing card = 1 point
playing card with diamonds = 2 points
playing card with 8 of diamonds = 3 points
playing card with 6 of diamonds = 1 point
(2 correct minus 1 incorrect)
playing card with 6 of hearts = -1 points
(1 correct minus 2 incorrect)
index card (not on table) = -2 points

6. Determine which team had the highest score.

Discussion

♦ How difficult was it to make observations of so many objects in so short a period of time?

♦ How did the loss of points for incorrect answers affect your descriptions?

♦ How accurate were your details?

♦ How could the team have improved its performance?

Closer Observation Worksheet

DESCRIPTION OF OBJECT	PTS.
TOTAL POINTS	

27 ◆ Data Directory

Objective

To develop effective team performance by producing a complete and accurate list of directory data while competing with other groups.

Group Size

Unlimited. Participants will work in groups with a maximum of six members each.

Time Required

Twenty to thirty minutes.

Materials

An identical copy of a telephone directory (a local or company directory), a prepared Data Directory Worksheet, and a pencil for each work group.

Preparation

Fill out your own specific directions for Page, Column, and Line items on the Data Directory Worksheet (i.e., where participants can find the information they need to capture the appropriate phone numbers for the Data Directory Worksheet), leaving the Number column blank, before duplicating copies for the participants. (It is recommended that the Line count not exceed 15.) Keep a copy of the list with the correct telephone numbers to use later when checking the groups' responses.

Process

1. Instruct the participants to form work groups of no more than six members each. Distribute a pencil, one copy of the selected telephone directory, and one Data

Directory Worksheet to each group. Explain that group members will take turns locating the information needed to complete the Data Directory Worksheet while competing against other groups.

2. When you give the signal, the first player of each team will open the directory to the page indicated, locate the appropriate column to use, and count down the entries as far as indicated. When the indicated entry is found, the player will record the telephone number on the worksheet. Then the person to his or her right is handed the directory, worksheet, and pencil. Proceeding in the same way, the second player finds the next telephone number and writes it down. The same process is repeated for the other numbers by the remaining players until the list is complete.

3. When the groups have completed the assignment, a representative from the team will bring the list to the facilitator, who will check it for accuracy. The first team to produce an accurate list is the winner.

Variation

Use computer data sheets or other technical data lists in place of a telephone directory. This is a good activity to use for reviewing data generated in a technical course.

Discussion

What made this task difficult? (Possible answers might relate to time pressures, losing count, transposing numbers.)

Lead a general discussion on problems relating to accuracy when using numbers and ways to prevent mistakes.

Data Directory Worksheet

PAGE	COLUMN	LINE	NUMBER

28 ◆ Food Chain Relay

Objective

To give participants an opportunity to work together in teams, under time pressure and while competing against other teams.

Group Size

Unlimited. Participants will work in teams with a maximum of six members each.

Time Required

Fifteen to twenty minutes.

Materials

A Food Chain Worksheet and a pencil for each group. (Have extra pencils on hand if needed.) Prizes for the winner(s) are optional.

Process

1. Divide the participants into work groups of no more than six members each. Distribute one copy of the Food Chain Worksheet and a pencil to each group. Ask each group to choose a member who will go first during the activity.

2. Explain that each group will attempt to list as many foods as possible on the worksheet, in alphabetical order, filling in a food item that corresponds to the letter on the worksheet. Play passes from one group member to the person on his or her left, like a relay race. All answers in column 1 must be attempted before column 2 can be started. For example, Player #1 fills in a food beginning with "A" in column 1, passes the sheet and pencil to Player #2, who fills in a food beginning with "B" (filling out the vertical column), and so on. Other members of the group may *not* make suggestions if a player cannot think of a word on his or

her turn. If a player cannot think of a word to represent the letter on his or her turn, an "X" should be placed in the block. Duplicate words are NOT allowed.

3. Play continues until all three columns have been filled or until the leader calls time. Teams will have five minutes to complete the task.

4. At the end of the allotted time, instruct teams to tally the total number of words entered on the worksheet. The team with the highest number of words is the winner. You may wish to present a prize to the winning team.

Discussion

♦ How did the time pressure affect the team's productivity?

♦ Did the task become more difficult by the time you reached the third column? Why?

♦ How did you feel if you were unable to find a word to match a particular letter?

♦ How supportive were other members of your group?

Food Chain Worksheet

	#1	#2	#3
A			
B			
C			
D			
E			
F			
G			
H			
I			
J			
K			
L			
M			
N			
O			
P			
Q			
R			
S			
T			
U			
V			
W			
X			
Y			
Z			

29 ♦ Four-by-Four

Objective

To give team members a chance to work together creatively and to reach consensus in developing conceptual connections.

Group Size

Unlimited. Participants will work in groups of five members or fewer.

Time Required

Twenty to thirty minutes.

Materials

A pencil and a Four-by-Four Worksheet for every participant; a flip chart; a felt-tip marker; a prize for the winning team (optional).

Note: You have been provided with one prepared chart for the activity, as well as one blank chart if you wish to provide your own designated word (or letters) and categories. If you use the blank chart instead of the prepared worksheet, you will need to provide a four-letter word (or four separate letters) to fill in the top row of the columns as well as four categories of your choosing for the left-hand column spaces. This information can be filled in on the worksheet before it is duplicated and distributed, or you can direct the participants to add the appropriate letters and words to their worksheets during the activity.

Process

1. Instruct participants to form groups with a maximum of five members each. Distribute the pencils and a Four-by-Four Worksheet to each participant.

2. Explain that the purpose of the game is to fill in the blanks on the worksheet with words that are appropriate for the categories indicated in the left column and that begin with each of the four letters at the top of the columns. Each group will work together to come up with one team word for each blank square.

3. Explain that each team will receive a score based on the following point system:

   ♦ 4 points for each entry your team selects that is not used by another team.

   ♦ 1 point for each entry you select that is also used by another team.

4. After the groups have completed filling in the worksheets, ask the teams to take turns sharing their answers with the reassembled large group, providing the word chosen for each category and letter. Using a marker and flip chart, tally the points scored by each team, according to the point system listed above. You may provide a small prize to the team with the highest total.

Discussion

Explain that the scoring system is designed to reward creativity and consensus thinking, both of which are needed for teams to be effective.

   ♦ Was it difficult for the team to come up with unusual answers? Why?

   ♦ Did any "rules" for participation apply in your team? If so, explain.

   ♦ How were conflicts handled?

Four-by-Four

	T	E	A	M
Vegetable				
Animal				
Bird				
River				

Four-by-Four

30 ♦ Goal Tending

Objective

To let participants work in groups to practice setting and achieving goals.

Group Size

A maximum of twenty-five participants, who will work in subgroups of six members or fewer.

Time Required

Twenty to thirty minutes.

Materials

A tennis ball; a wastebasket; a chair; index cards (one card for each subgroup); felt-tip markers (one marker of a different color for each group); masking tape; a flip chart.

Preparation

In the meeting room, place a wastebasket approximately eight feet away from a designated starting point (which you can mark with masking tape on the floor). Place a chair three feet in front of the wastebasket (five feet from the starting point).

Process

1. Explain to the participants that after subgroups are formed, the chosen representatives of each team will attempt to bounce a tennis ball *in front* of the chair so that it clears the chair and drops into the wastebasket.

2. Divide the entire group into at least two teams with a maximum of six members each. Distribute one index card and a felt-tip marker to each group (each group should receive a separate color marker for identification purposes). Explain the following rules:

> (1) Each team will select two representative players.
>
> (2) Each player will have three chances to bounce the ball so that it goes into the wastebasket. Each player will be allowed one practice shot *before* the actual "tournament" begins.
>
> (3) Each team needs to set a goal based on the total number of successful shots it anticipates making (e.g., 2 players × 3 balls = 6 total attempts per team). Stress that the goal should be realistic, yet challenging. Allow the teams a few minutes to choose their representative players and to set goals. Each group should record its goal on the index card provided.

3. Collect the cards, which you will use to post the groups' goals later. Next, start the game by instructing the two designated players from each team to throw the tennis ball three times per representative player. Note the number of successful attempts on the flip chart and record the total for each team.

4. Compare the stated goal and the number of successful throws for each team. Report the results by recording the team color, the goal, and the actual successful attempts on the flip chart.

Discussion

♦ How well did you do in accomplishing your goal?

♦ How did you determine who would represent the team?

♦ How did you determine the goal?

31 ♦ Gridlock

Objective

To experience gridlock as participants try to exchange assigned places with their teammates.

Group Size

Unlimited, but at least sixteen participants are recommended (the total number of participants should be divisible by eight or ten).

Time Required

Twenty to thirty minutes.

Materials

Construction paper (8.5" × 11" white stock and colored stock). You will need one white sheet for each participant and one colored sheet for each work group. Masking tape may be used to secure the paper to the floor.

Process

1. Instruct participants to form work groups of eight or ten members each and to divide each work group into two equal teams (i.e., a work group of eight members would create two teams of four members; a work group of ten members would create two teams of five members). For each group, place eight or ten sheets of white paper (depending on the number of players) in a line on the floor with one colored sheet in the center and the white sheets on the outside. The diagram below shows the setup for a team with ten members that has been divided into two work groups of five members each.

☐ ☐ ☐ ☐ ☐ ■ ☐ ☐ ☐ ☐ ☐

2. Instruct each member of the two groups to stand on a sheet of white paper, facing the middle unoccupied square represented by the colored sheet. Explain that the purpose of the activity is to have the two groups exchange places on the line of rectangles. All members to the left of the vacant center rectangle (the sheet of colored paper) must end up on the right side, and vice versa.

3. Explain the rules for moving legally and illegally. Using the following moves, describe how the two groups can attempt to exchange places legally:

   (1) A member may move into any empty space directly in front of him or her.

   (2) A member may move around a member from the other group into an empty space.

   Then explain the following illegal moves:

   (1) A member may not move backwards.

   (2) A member may not move around a member facing the same direction.

   (3) Two members may not move at the same time.

4. Start the gridlock game and monitor the teams' progress.

Discussion

♦ What factors influenced your ability to perform this activity?

♦ How were decisions to move handled?

♦ Did any conflicts arise?

♦ What could have been done differently to improve the process?

32 ♦ Hand It Over

Objective

To cooperate with other team members by passing peanuts along a line of participants while keeping hands clasped.

Group Size

Unlimited. Participants will work in groups of up to ten members each.

Time Required

Ten minutes.

Materials

Peanuts (unshelled, ten for each subgroup) and chairs (two for each subgroup).

Process

1. Instruct participants to form work groups of up to ten members each.

2. Have each team stand in a line. Position a chair at each end of the line. Place ten peanuts on one of the chairs for each team. Direct each of the team players to grasp the hands of the players on either side.

3. Explain that the peanuts are to be passed, one at a time, from player to player until they are all transferred to the chair at the end of the line. The passing of peanuts must be accomplished while all the participants are clasping hands, which must be kept joined from the beginning to the end of the line.

4. Start the process. When all groups have accomplished the task, reassemble the entire group for discussion questions.

Discussion

♦ How easy was it for the group members to keep their hands grasped during the exercise?

♦ How do we equate this activity to a team's interdependence?

33 ♦ Hidden Hands

Objective

To give participants practice in communicating with other team members and in making group decisions while sequencing a comic strip.

Group Size

Unlimited. Participants will work in groups of three to four members each.

Time Required

Twenty to thirty minutes.

Materials

A comic strip from the Sunday paper (duplicated so each work group has a copy); one envelope for each subgroup.

Preparation

Photocopy enough copies of the comic strip to provide one for each work group. Cut each strip into separate panels and place the panels in an envelope.

Process

1. Instruct the participants to form work groups of three to four members each. Distribute one envelope containing a set of comic strip panels to each team.

2. Direct the members of each team to open the envelope, place the panels of the comic strip face down without examining them, and shuffle them around the table.

3. While the panels are on the table face down, hidden from view, members of each team take turns drawing a panel (without showing it to others), going around until all panels have been chosen. Team members are allowed to describe their own panels as fully as possible, but they are not allowed to look at the panels of the other participants or to show their panels to others.

4. When the team members have agreed on which panel is first in the cartoon (based on the participants' descriptions of the panels), they place it face down on the table. After they have placed all the panels face down in the order they have determined, they then turn them over to see if they have sequenced the comic in the proper order.

Discussion

Lead a discussion on the communication process used to describe the panels and the means by which group decisions were made. Explore ways in which members of the group could have improved the team's performance.

34 ♦ Imagine That

Objective

To encourage participants to practice creative thinking by responding to unusual questions.

Group Size

Unlimited.

Time Required

Twenty to thirty minutes.

Materials

Imagine That Worksheets and pencils (one for each participant).

Process

1. Distribute one copy of the Imagine That Worksheet to each participant. Explain that individuals should use their imagination to answer each of the ten questions as fully and descriptively as possible.

2. Allow approximately five minutes for this part of the activity to be accomplished.

3. When the participants have finished, ask them to gather into small work groups. The group members should discuss their answers, giving some reasons why they responded as they did.

Discussion

♦ Which questions were the most difficult to answer? Why?

♦ Were there many similarities between one person's answer and others in the group?

♦ Did other members in your group have difficulty making a connection between your imagery and the concept? Why?

♦ How do we use similar descriptions in our everyday communication?

♦ How does creativity help in problem-solving strategies?

Imagine That Worksheet

1. What shape is a WISH?

2. What color is TODAY?

3. What temperature is your CAREER?

4. What does a HUG sound like?

5. What does your favorite SONG feel like?

6. What does QUALITY smell like?

7. What does HAPPINESS taste like?

8. How much does ANGER weigh?

9. What is the distance of your LIFE?

10. What is the texture of SUCCESS?

35 ◆ In Search Of

Objective

To give participants an opportunity to work together cooperatively in groups by locating hidden words in a scrambled letter puzzle.

Group Size

Unlimited. Participants will work in groups with a maximum of five members each.

Time Required

Fifteen minutes.

Materials

A pencil and one copy each of the In Search of Word List, Word Search Puzzle, and In Search of Answer Sheet for each work group. Prizes for the winning team are optional.

Process

1. Instruct participants to form work groups of no more than five members each and to choose a team recorder for the end of the activity when the answers are checked. Distribute a pencil and one copy each of the In Search of Word List and Word Search Puzzle to each group.

2. Explain that the members of each team will work together to locate twenty words hidden within the Word Search Puzzle. The team that finds the most words correctly in the shortest amount of time will be the winner. Stress that all teams should continue with the task until all groups have finished.

3. The contest will begin with one player examining the Word Search Puzzle in an attempt to locate one of the words listed on the In Search of Word List. When a word is found, it is circled on the Word Search Puzzle and crossed off the Word List. Then the pencil and both worksheets are passed to the player on the right, who continues the process. The process is repeated until all words have been found and the team members raise their hands to indicate that they have completed the challenge. The time of completion should be noted by the facilitator and team members should be directed to lower their hands.

4. Start the group challenge. After all teams have completed the activity, distribute a copy of the In Search of Answer Sheet to each group. Each team's recorder should check the group puzzle for accuracy and the number of correct words. The team with the highest number of correct words and the shortest completion time is declared the winner. You may wish to distribute a small prize to each team member.

In Search Of Word List

Locate the following words in the Word Search Puzzle:

CREATIVE	QUALITY
DEPEND	RELATIONS
EFFICIENCY	SERVICE
GOALS	SKILLS
GROUP	TALENTS
GROWTH	TASK
HELP	TEAMWORK
LEAD	TRAINING
LISTEN	VALUES
MISSION	VISION

In Search of - Puzzle

```
E  U  F  S  G  R  O  W  T  H
P  L  E  H  I  U  Q  E  D  O
D  E  P  E  N  D  U  S  S  A
S  A  K  R  O  T  A  L  E  R
N  M  R  N  W  H  L  A  O  I
O  G  O  E  C  I  I  O  I  T
I  S  W  T  K  D  T  G  T  A
T  T  M  S  L  E  Y  D  A  R
A  F  A  I  E  L  I  X  E  K
L  H  E  L  R  U  A  L  R  M
E  G  T  X  E  J  L  V  C  I
R  R  O  K  F  N  M  A  G  S
D  O  A  P  F  Y  T  N  V  S
A  U  V  E  I  R  I  S  L  I
Q  P  N  K  C  N  L  E  A  O
N  O  I  S  I  V  A  R  E  N
T  S  D  A  E  D  U  V  R  F
B  A  R  W  N  E  Q  I  Y  T
L  T  S  I  C  T  V  C  E  S
E  T  O  K  Y  R  T  E  S  V
```

In Search Of – Answer Sheet

```
E  U  F  S  G  R  O  W  T  H
P  L  E  H  I  U  Q  E  D  O
D  E  P  E  N  D  Q  U  A  A
S  A  K  R  O  T  A  L  S  R
N  M  R  N  W  H  L  A  O  I
O  G  O  E  C  I  I  O  G  T
I  S  W  T  K  D  T  G  D  A
T  F  M  I  L  E  Y  D  X  R
A  H  A  L  R  U  I  X  L  K
L  G  E  X  E  J  A  L  V  M
E  R  T  K  F  N  L  V  A  I
R  O  O  P  F  Y  M  A  N  S
D  U  A  E  I  R  T  N  S  S
A  P  V  N  C  N  I  S  E  I
Q  N  N  S  I  A  E  R  A  O
N  O  I  S  I  V  D  R  V  N
T  S  D  A  E  N  U  V  I  F
B  A  R  W  N  E  Q  I  C  T
L  T  S  I  C  T  V  C  E  S
E  T  O  K  Y  R  E  S  V
```

36 ◆ Just Like...

Objective

To give participants practice in using descriptive analogies to describe team characteristics.

Group Size

Unlimited. Participants will form work groups with a maximum of five members each.

Time Required

Fifteen to twenty minutes.

Materials

One Analogy Card, a blank sheet of paper, and a pencil for each work group; a flip chart and a felt-tip marker (optional).

Preparation

Duplicate each page (two pages total) of the Analogy Cards on a separate sheet of card stock and cut into individual cards following the dashed lines. Each page provides different analogies for six groups.

Process

1. Instruct participants to form work groups with a maximum of five members each. Distribute a sheet of blank paper, a pencil, and one Analogy Card to each group.

2. Direct the groups to come up with six examples of their analogy to describe their current work group and to write them on the sheet of paper.

Variations

1. Instead of giving each group one Analogy Card, you can give each group one set of six different Analogy Cards. Direct the groups to write one example for each analogy and to describe their reasons.

2. When working with a small total group (ten or fewer participants): Announce (or display on a flip chart) one Analogy Card to the entire group. Using a round-robin method, have each member of the group give an example of the analogy and explain his or her reasoning. This procedure may be repeated with additional Analogy Cards.

Discussion

Analogies are shared and reasonings discussed with the reassembled group.

Analogy Cards

Our TEAM is like
PEANUT BUTTER
AND JELLY
because....

Our TEAM is like a
HIGH SCHOOL
REUNION
because....

Our TEAM is like a
BOX OF CEREAL
because....

Our TEAM is like a
LUXURY CAR
because....

Our TEAM is like a
SUPERMARKET
because....

Our TEAM is like a
BREAKFAST CEREAL
because....

Analogy Cards

Our TEAM is like a
BOAT
because....

Our TEAM is like a
WATERFALL
because....

Our TEAM is like
ICE CREAM
because....

Our TEAM is like a
VOLCANO
because....

Our TEAM is like a
HOUSE
because....

Our TEAM is like a
RAILROAD
because....

37 ◆ Keys to Success

Objective

To provide participants with an opportunity to work with other team members to locate two matching key symbols in a hidden puzzle.

Group Size

Unlimited. Participants will work in groups with a maximum of four members each.

Time Required

Fifteen to twenty minutes.

Materials

A pencil and one copy of the Keys to Success Worksheet for each work group. The facilitator needs a copy of the Keys to Success Solution Sheet (you may also want to put the solution sheet on an overhead transparency if you want to show it to all participants at the same time).

Process

1. Instruct participants to form work groups with a maximum of four members each. Distribute a pencil and one copy of the Keys to Success Worksheet to each group.

2. Explain that the picture puzzle on the worksheet shows a wide variety of keys, but only two of the keys match exactly. The challenge for each group is to locate these two identical keys and to circle them. The team that solves the puzzle in the least amount of time will be declared the winner.

3. As the work groups complete the puzzle, a representative from each group should bring the worksheet to the facilitator, who will note the time of completion and check the group's worksheet for accuracy using the Keys to Success Solution Sheet. Groups will have a maximum of ten minutes to complete the task.

4. Call "TIME" after 10 minutes if all groups have not finished. Indicate the correct answers by using an overhead transparency of the solution or by describing the location of the correct keys. Determine the winning team by soliciting completion times, closing the range downward. For example, you can ask, "Who finished in less than eight minutes?" "...less than seven minutes?" etc., until the shortest time is indicated.

Discussion

♦ How did your group attempt to find the matching keys?

♦ How would you improve your procedure next time?

Keys to Success Worksheet

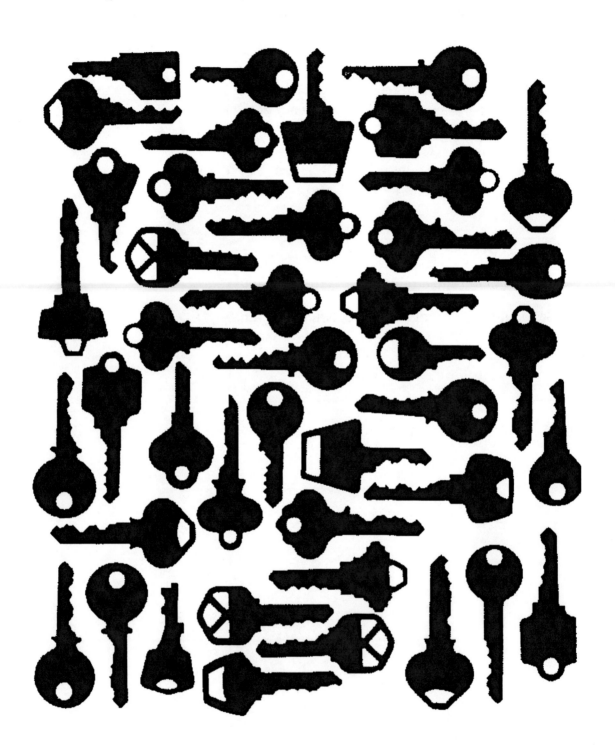

Keys to Success Solution Sheet

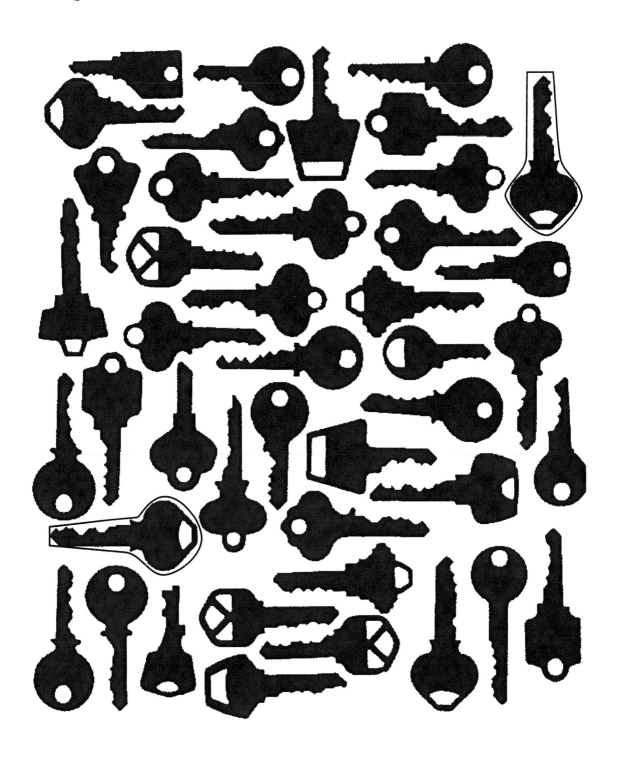

38 ◆ Last Straw

Objective

To give participants an opportunity to work together in a challenging activity in which they pass objects from player to player.

Group Size

Unlimited. Participants will form work groups with a maximum of twelve members.

Time Required

Ten to fifteen minutes.

Materials

One straw and one paper cup for each participant; a large quantity of dried navy beans.

Note: Other objects may be substituted for the dried beans, but some experimenting beforehand should be done to ensure safety and applicability.

Process

1. Form the participants into teams, each consisting of a maximum of twelve members.

2. Direct each team to stand in a line. Distribute one cup and one straw to each participant. Explain that the teams will compete against each other in a relay race.

3. Place ten dried navy beans (or other objects) into the cup of the first player on each team. Explain that all the beans must be transferred from this cup to the

next player's cup by inhaling the beans through the straw and removing them one bean at a time. The second player must wait until all the beans have been transferred to his or her cup before beginning the transfer process to the next player's cup.

4. The procedure continues until all the beans have been transferred to the end of the line, as rapidly as possible. The first team to complete the challenge is declared the winner.

Variations

1. Ask each team to stand in a circle instead of a line and to continue the transfer procedure until all the beans have been returned to the first player's cup.

2. Allow players to pass the beans simultaneously, rather than waiting for each player to transfer all ten beans to the next player's cup before continuing with the transfer process.

Discussion

Discuss how the time pressure affected each group's performance.

39 ♦ No Vowels Allowed

Objective

To give participants the opportunity to practice cooperation in a spelling bee, using prescribed motions in place of vowels.

Group Size

A maximum of twenty-five participants.

Time Required

Twenty minutes.

Materials

A list of spelling words prepared by the facilitator.

Note: It is recommended that you limit the length of the chosen words to approximately five to seven letters. This is a good activity to use for reviewing words related to specific course content.

Process

1. Instruct participants to stand in a line so that a spelling bee can be conducted.

2. Explain that each player will be assigned a word to spell, except that some very special rules apply to the method of spelling the words. No player is permitted to pronounce any vowel; each time a vowel occurs, a prescribed motion is to be substituted. The rules for substituting vowels are as follows (you should describe as well as demonstrate each signal):

Instead of	A:	raise your right hand
	E:	raise your left hand
	I:	point to one eye
	O:	point to your mouth
	U:	point to any other player

Each player who "spells" the word correctly remains standing. If a player fails to spell a word correctly, he or she must sit down. A failure occurs for any of the following circumstances:

♦ A vowel is pronounced.

♦ An incorrect substitute is given for a vowel.

♦ The word is misspelled.

Play continues until one player remains, or until time is called.

40 ◆ Picture Perfect

Objective

To give participants an opportunity to work in teams to compare and contrast the details of two similar pictures.

Group Size

Unlimited. Participants will work in groups with a maximum of four members each.

Time Required

Ten to fifteen minutes.

Materials

One Picture Perfect A Handout, one Picture Perfect B Handout, a blank sheet of paper, and a pencil for each participant.

Process

1. Instruct participants to form work groups with a maximum of four members in each group. Explain that participants will work with their groups in a team effort to compare the details of two very similar pictures (one of which they will see for only two minutes).

2. Distribute one copy of the Picture Perfect A Handout, a blank sheet of paper, and a pencil to each participant. Explain that group members will have only two minutes to study the picture for details before working with their groups.

3. Announce start and stop times, allowing two minutes for the study process. After calling time, collect the pictures from all participants.

4. Distribute one copy of the Picture Perfect B Handout to each participant. In their teams, group members are to compile a list of details that describe the differences between Picture A, which they studied earlier for two minutes, and Picture B. Allow approximately five minutes for the groups to work together.

5. Redistribute the Picture Perfect A Handouts for groups to compare their answers. Provide the following solutions and have each team determine its number of correct answers.

Solution

(1) "B" taxi driver has no mustache.

(2) The girl's hair is different.

(3) "B" left building has an additional floor on it.

(4) The lines are on different sides of the center building.

(5) "B" small building on right has windows.

(6) "B" taxi hubcaps have no spokes.

(7) "B" taxi tag is 141; "A" taxi tag is 147.

(8) Grille on the taxi has different spacing ("B" is narrow).

(9) The top of the building on the right of traffic light is different.

(10) "B" taxi has two headlights instead of four.

(11) "B" back vehicle is missing a second figure.

(12) "B" back vehicle has two domes instead of one.

(13) "B" back vehicle has a round headlight instead of a rectangle.

(14) "B" boy has no eyeglasses.

(15) "B" boy has no freckles.

(16) "B" taxi is missing a handle.

(17) "B" taxi has a strip on the side.

(18) "B" taxi side mirror is square instead of round.

(19) "B" taxi has a back bumper.

(20) "B" traffic light extension at top is missing.

Discussion

♦ How difficult was this task?

♦ How could the team have improved its performance?

Picture Perfect Handout A

Picture Perfect Handout B

41 ◆ Poem's Progress

Objective

To work in teams creating progressive rhyming poems.

Group Size

Unlimited. Participants will work in groups with a maximum of six members each.

Time Required

Ten to fifteen minutes.

Materials

A blank sheet of paper and a pencil for each participant.

Process

1. Instruct participants to form work groups with a maximum of six members in each. Distribute one sheet of paper and a pencil to each participant. Explain that each group will use a team effort to create a set of rhyming poems.

2. Direct each player to write the first line of a verse at the top of the sheet of paper. The verse can be either a quotation from a well-known poem or one that the individual composes for this purpose.

3. When all participants have written a line of verse on their papers, they should fold the paper so that the line cannot be seen, and then they should copy the last word of the line of verse so that only it is visible below the fold.

4. Next, each participant should hand over his or her paper to the individual on his or her right. This player then writes a second line on the sheet ending with a

word that rhymes with the word that is visible below the fold of the sheet (the last word of the first line of verse). The paper is folded again, with the last word of the second line written below the fold. Again the paper is handed to the next person on the right, and this player repeats the procedure.

5. This process continues until all group members have had an opportunity to write a line for the poem begun by each person in the group. The result is a group of poems in which all the lines rhyme (i.e., four-member teams will create four poems with four lines each, and so on).

6. Each person should read aloud the poem that he or she holds. Depending on the total number of participants and the time available, this may be done within the individual work groups or with the reassembled group as an audience.

42 ◆ Quote Cubes

Objective

To work together in teams to discover a quotation by unscrambling letters in a puzzle.

Group Size

Unlimited. Participants will work in groups with a maximum of five members in each.

Time Required

Fifteen to twenty minutes.

Materials

A pencil and a Quote Cubes Worksheet for each participant.

Process

1. Instruct participants to form work groups with a maximum of five members in each. Distribute one copy of the Quote Cubes Worksheet and a pencil to each person. Tell the groups that they will work together to solve a puzzle that reveals a quotation.

2. Explain that the letters over each vertical column on the worksheet should be placed—not necessarily in the original listed order—into the empty spaces below them. Black squares indicate ends of words; a word without a black square at the end of a line is continued on the next line. If all letters have been placed correctly, a lengthy quotation is revealed when the words are read left to right, line by line.

3. Allow approximately ten minutes for the groups to work together to solve the quotation, and then ask a volunteer to give the solution.

Solution

"The failure of past efforts can provide valuable clues to a future course of action."

Discussion

♦ How did you approach the task?

♦ How did the size of the group affect its decision making?

♦ How can we apply the quotation to problem-solving activities, such as this one?

Quote Cubes Worksheet

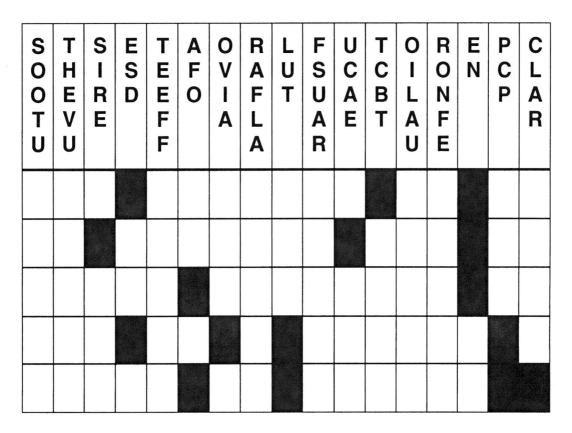

Solution:

43 ◆ Rhymed Riddles

Objective

To give participants the opportunity to work together in groups to create two-word rhymes and turn them into riddles for other groups to solve.

Group Size

Up to thirty participants, who will work in subgroups of up to six members each.

Time Required

Ten to fifteen minutes.

Materials

Blank sheets of paper and pencils for every participant. A flip chart and felt-tip markers are optional if the facilitator wants to post the riddle process and examples.

Process

1. Instruct participants to form work groups with up to six members in each group.

2. Distribute blank sheets of paper and pencils to group members. Explain that participants will work in their groups creating riddles for other groups to solve. The answer to each riddle will consist of a two-word rhyme. Describe the following riddle procedure (you may also wish to post the procedure on a flip chart), using the example below:

    (1) List four nouns (e.g., cup).

(2) List as many rhyming words as possible that can be associated with each noun (e.g., for the noun "cup," rhyming words are pup, sup, up).

(3) Create a riddle for each two-word rhyme (e.g., What is a dish for a young dog? Answer: "Pup Cup").

3. After subgroups have worked together creating two-word rhymes and riddles, each subgroup takes turns reading its favorite riddle out loud, and the other subgroups try to solve it. If time allows, additional rounds of riddles may be played.

44 ◆ Scrambled Sense

Objective

To learn how communication affects team work by constructing sentences through traded word cards without speaking.

Group Size

Unlimited. Participants will work in groups of four members each.

Time Required

Fifteen to twenty minutes.

Materials

One complete set of Scrambled Sense Cards (in envelopes marked #1-4) for *each* work group.

Preparation

Duplicate each sheet (four pages total) of the Scrambled Sense Cards on card stock and cut each sheet into individual pieces along the dashed lines. Prepare one set of four envelopes for *each* work group:

One set = Envelopes #1-4 with the following cards:

Envelope #1: the, dogs, brown, I'm, shining

Envelope #2: the, sun, barking, hair, store

Envelope #3: child, is, very, going, loudly

Envelope #4: the, started, to, has, brightly

Process

1. Instruct participants to form work groups of four members each. Distribute one complete set of envelopes (#1-4) to each team, handing one envelope to each person in the group.

2. Explain that teams will be given ten minutes to accomplish their assignment, which is for each person on the team to create one meaningful sentence consisting of five words using the words provided in the four envelopes. At the end of the ten-minute period, each team player should have one five-word sentence formed in front of him or her using the word cards in the envelopes.

3. Explain the RULES of the activity:

   Players on a team may exchange cards if they wish, *but no member may speak*. No team member can indicate in any way that he or she wants a card belonging to another player; participants must wait until it is presented to them before taking it. Team players must accept a card from another team player any time it is presented to them. Participants may offer their own cards to other members of their team at any time.

Solution

At the end of the ten-minute time period, call "TIME" and present the following sentence solutions to the groups:

> I'm going to the store.
>
> The sun is shining brightly.
>
> The child has brown hair.
>
> Dogs started barking very loudly.

Discussion

♦ How difficult was this task? Why?

♦ How does communication affect the way in which we work together?

Scrambled Sense Cards – Envelope #1

THE

DOGS

BROWN

I'M

SHINING

THE

SUN

BARKING

HAIR

STORE

Scrambled Sense Cards – Envelope #3

CHILD

IS

EVERY

GOING

LOUDLY

Scrambled Sense Cards – Envelope #4

THE	**STARTED**
TO	**HAS**
BRIGHTLY	

45 ◆ Sock Search

Objective

To work in groups competing against other teams in a modified version of a scavenger hunt (locating specific items contained in a sock).

Group Size

A maximum of thirty participants, who will work in groups of up to ten members each.

Time Required

Fifteen to twenty minutes.

Materials

Large tube socks, each filled identically with fifteen or more assorted small items (e.g., buttons, hairpins, marbles, paper clips, pens, pencils); one filled sock is needed for each work group. The facilitator needs to keep a list of the items placed in the socks in the order in which they will be drawn.

Preparation

Prepare the tube socks and a list of the fifteen items used to fill the socks, listing them in the order that they will be located and removed by the participants. The number of items to find will depend on how many players are assigned to each team and the time available.

Process

1. Instruct participants to form teams of no more than ten members each and to select a team leader. Have each team form a line with the designated leader facing the remaining members, who stand one behind the other.

2. Give each team's designated leader one of the filled socks. Explain that the teams will compete with each other to be the first to complete the assigned task. The team leader will hold the sock that contains a variety of small items. When the group facilitator announces the first item to be located, the first team player (facing the team leader who holds the sock) is to locate that object in the sock. After the item is located, the team player should take it to the announcer (the facilitator), who will tell the player the next item on the list to be located. The player will deliver this message to the next team player on his or her team, who will advance to the team leader holding the sock and locate that object (the team player who just located the item in the sock should move to the end of his or her team's line). Play continues until one team completes the entire list of items to be drawn.

   Note: It is important that each team player hand over the located object to the announcer (facilitator) so that the next assigned item from the list can be determined.

46 ♦ Team Challenge

Objective

To enable groups to use problem-solving strategies to solve a sequential word puzzle.

Group Size

Unlimited. Participants will work in groups with a maximum of four members each.

Time Required

Fifteen to twenty minutes.

Materials

One Team Challenge Worksheet and a pencil for each participant.

Process

1. Instruct participants to form work groups of no more than four members each.

2. Distribute one copy of the Team Challenge Worksheet and a pencil to each participant. Explain that each group will have five minutes to find a solution to the puzzle:

   > By changing only *one* of the four letters each time the letters are entered in the next vertical column (working from left to right), the group should form three words that will transform SPOT (on the left column) into TEAM (on the right column).

3. After five minutes, have each group in turn share its answer with the other groups. Then compare the solutions for similarities and differences.

Variation

Allow ten to fifteen minutes for each work group to come up with as many *different* solutions as possible in the specified time period. The team with the most solutions is the winner.

Solution

Although there are many possibilities, one solution to the Team Challenge is shown below:

S	S	S	S	T
P	P	E	E	E
O	A	A	A	A
T	T	T	M	M

Discussion

◆ How did the group approach the problem?

◆ Since there is no one single answer, how did the group decide on which words to use?

◆ How did the time pressure affect group dynamics?

Team Challenge Worksheet

By changing only *one* of the four letters each time you fill out the next vertical column (working from left to right), form three words that will transform SPOT into TEAM.

S				T
P				E
O				A
T				M

47 ◆ Team Hats

Objective

To strengthen a group's identity and encourage team work as group members make team hats that convey a common theme.

Group Size

Unlimited. Participants will work in groups with a maximum of six members each.

Time Required

Twenty to thirty minutes.

Materials

Every group needs enough materials to create a hat for each group member: white painter's caps; a variety of marking pens or paint; assorted scrap material (fabric, sequins, feathers, etc.); fasteners (glue, staplers, tape, brads, clips).

Process

1. Place all the hat-making materials on a table in a central location, accessible to everyone.

2. Instruct participants to form work groups of no more than six members each.

3. Explain that a team forms its identity by defining itself in a unique way. In this group challenge, each team will work together to create "team hats" for every member of the team using the materials provided. Stress that all the hats from one team may not necessarily be identical, but there should be either a common theme or one thing that distinguishes one team's hats from the hats of another team.

4. Allow sufficient time for the activity to be completed, then direct participants to wear their hats as you lead a general discussion of the exercise.

Variation

Instead of white painter's caps, use construction paper, poster board, or corrugated cardboard to make the hats.

Discussion

Lead a general discussion on how teams unite to work toward a common goal (common theme of hats) while utilizing a diversity of skills and talents (differences in hats). You may wish to emphasize that team work is a matter of "putting your heads together" to get the job done.

48 ♦ Tic-Tactical-Toe

Objective

To work in teams to find the best way of duplicating a set of materials that can be viewed for only a short period of time.

Group Size

Unlimited. Participants will work in groups with a maximum of six members each.

Time Required

Twenty to thirty minutes.

Materials

One tic-tac-toe board for each work group; duplicates of the different play items used on the board (which participants will have to find during the activity); a cloth to cover one tic-tac-toe board; masking tape; wide felt-tip marker.

Note: The location in which the activity takes place will determine the board items to be used, because participants will need to find duplicate items to place on their boards. For example, in a traditional training room, items such as staplers, scissors, and felt-tip markers may be chosen; whereas in a conference meeting room you may need to substitute items that can be found in a participant's possession (pens, nail files, wallets, sunglasses, pennies, etc.).

Preparation

Make enough tic-tac-toe boards to accommodate each work group (one board for each group) plus one for the facilitator. Using poster board and a wide, black felt-tip marker or masking tape, mark the board with a tic-tac-toe design as shown:

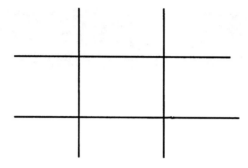

Place the nine items (one in each space) on the facilitator's board and cover the board with a cloth so participants cannot see it. If desired, you may wish to place some of the duplicate items in *obscure* places around the room.

Process

1. Instruct the participants to form work groups of up to six members each. Distribute one tic-tac-toe board to each group.

2. Explain that the teams will be given a very brief opportunity to view a set of materials on a tic-tac-toe board that they will attempt to duplicate and position appropriately on their own tic-tac-toe boards.

3. Uncover the facilitator's board and allow the participants to view the materials for a very brief period of time, about ten or fifteen seconds. Replace the cover on the board. Tell the teams that they will have fifteen minutes to complete the task (by finding similar items and placing them on their boards in the same position as on the original board).

4. When the time has expired, have each team observe the completed boards of the other work groups and compare them to the original board.

Discussion

♦ How close did you come to duplicating the materials and their positions on your board?

♦ What kinds of substitutions did you use? (e.g., a blue pen instead of a red pen)

♦ Did you need to rely on resources obtained from other groups?

49 ◆ Tribal Adventure

Objective

To practice problem solving in groups using analytical reasoning to solve a logic puzzle.

Group Size

Unlimited. Participants will work in groups with a maximum of four members each.

Time Required

Twenty to thirty minutes.

Materials

Pencils and one Tribal Adventure Worksheet for each work group; a flip chart (or a transparency sheet and an overhead projector); a felt-tip marker.

Process

1. Direct participants to form work groups of four members or fewer. Distribute one copy of the Tribal Adventure Worksheet to each participant.

2. Briefly review the group challenge and explain that each group will have approximately fifteen minutes to work together to answer the four questions asked at the bottom of the worksheet.

3. Tell the groups to begin their assignment and give them a two-minute warning.

4. After the groups have finished (or when the time has run out), record each group's solution on a flip chart or on an overhead transparency. Review the correct solution using the information provided below.

Solution

What tribe does **Coffi** belong to?	*Crocodile*
What tribe does **Damu** belong to?	*Koala*
What tribe does **Ena** belong to?	*Kangaroo*
What tribe does **Bolu** belong to?	*Kangaroo*

Every member of the Kangaroo Tribe always tells the truth. Coffi, who says he is not a Kangaroo, cannot be a Kangaroo, whether he is telling the truth or not.

Since every member of the Koala tribe always lies, Coffi, who says he is not a Kangaroo, cannot be a Koala. Coffi must therefore be a Crocodile.

Ena cannot be a Crocodile, because Coffi is the Crocodile. Therefore Ena, who says he is not a Crocodile, must be telling the truth. He cannot be a lying Koala, so he must be a truthful Kangaroo.

Bolu, therefore, must be a Kangaroo also because truthful Ena says so. That leaves Damu as the Koala.

Discussion

♦ Describe the group's problem-solving approach.

♦ How well received were individual participant's ideas or suggestions?

♦ Did any conflicts arise? How were they handled?

♦ Did some members feel "left out" during the process? Why?

Tribal Adventure Worksheet

An adventurer goes to Australia to locate an Aborigine scout named Bolu, but he doesn't know to which tribe Bolu belongs. There are three tribes in the area: the Kangaroo Tribe, the Koala Tribe, and the Crocodile Tribe.

A person who belongs to the Kangaroo Tribe always tells the truth.

A person who belongs to the Koala Tribe always lies.

A person who belongs to the Crocodile Tribe sometimes tells the truth and sometimes lies.

In order to find Bolu, the adventurer must determine the correct tribe. He asks three Aborigines—each from a different tribe—two questions:

"What tribe do you belong to?

"What tribe does Bolu belong to?"

Coffi answers: "I am not a Kangaroo. Bolu is a Koala."

Damu says: "I am not a Koala. Bolu is a Crocodile."

Ena says: "I am not a Crocodile. Bolu is a Kangaroo."

Solution

What tribe does **Coffi** belong to? _____

What tribe does **Damu** belong to? _____

What tribe does **Ena** belong to? _____

What tribe does **Bolu** belong to? _____

50 ♦ Trivial Numbers

Objective

To work in teams to reach group consensus on answers to assorted trivia questions.

Group Size

Unlimited. Participants will work in groups with a maximum of six members each.

Time Required

Twenty minutes.

Materials

A pencil and one Trivial Numbers Questionnaire for each participant.

Process

1. Instruct participants to form work groups of up to six members each. Distribute one copy of the Trivial Numbers Questionnaire and a pencil to each person.

2. Explain that the groups will be playing a game similar to Trivial Pursuit®. The six categories listed all require an answer involving a number. The group with the most correct "Team" answers will be the winner.

3. Explain that the first step is to have each participant attempt to answer the questions, placing responses in the "Self" column of the questionnaire. Allow sufficient time for this step to be completed.

4. Next, explain that each group will be allowed ten minutes to discuss the questions and come to an agreement on a "Team" answer, which is to be listed

on the appropriate line in that column. The answer chosen by the group must be agreed on by *all* members of the team, and majority voting is not allowed. Call "TIME" after 10 minutes.

5. When groups have completed the questionnaires and reached their team answers, provide the solutions.

Solution

Geography	7 zones
Entertainment	10 lords
History	21st Amendment
Art & Literature	20 years
Science & Nature	4 wings
Sports & Leisure	40 spaces

Discussion

♦ How difficult was this task?

♦ How were conflicts handled in your group?

Trivial Numbers Questionnaire

	Self	**Team**

Geography

How many time zones are there in Canada?   _____   _____

Entertainment

How many "lords a-leaping" are there in the
Twelve Days of Christmas carol?   _____   _____

History

What amendment to the U.S. Constitution
ended Prohibition?   _____   _____

Art & Literature

How many years did Rip Van Winkle sleep?   _____   _____

Science & Nature

How many wings does a bee have?   _____   _____

Sports & Leisure

How many spaces are there on a Monopoly® board?   _____   _____

51 ♦ Visual Effects

Objective

To work creatively in teams to solve a series of word puzzles.

Group Size

Unlimited. Participants work in groups with a maximum of six members each.

Time Required

Ten to fifteen minutes.

Materials

A pencil, one Visual Effects Puzzle Sheet, and one Visual Effects Worksheet for each participant.

Process

1. Direct participants to form work groups of up to six members each. Distribute a pencil, a Visual Effects Puzzle Sheet, and a Visual Effects Worksheet to each participant.

2. Explain that each team will have five minutes to determine the familiar saying represented by each puzzle on the Visual Effects Puzzle Sheet. Answers should be written on the Visual Effects Worksheet provided to the participants. Tell everyone to begin the activity.

3. Call "TIME" after five minutes have elapsed. Review the participants' answers by asking for audience input on each puzzle in sequence.

Solution

    (1) Life has its ups and downs.

    (2) One step forward, two steps back.

    (3) Having it both ways.

    (4) Gross injustice.

    (5) You ought to be in pictures.

    (6) The good, the bad, and the ugly.

    (7) A cut above the rest.

    (8) Backseat driver.

    (9) For once in your life.

    (10) Painting by numbers.

    (11) Friends in high places.

    (12) One fine day.

    (13) Turn the clocks back.

    (14) Lie in wait.

    (15) Forty winks.

Discussion

♦ How did perceptions play a role in solving these puzzles? (*People look at things in different ways.*)

♦ How can these kinds of puzzles help stimulate creative thinking? (*They show that there is more than one way to view things.*)

Visual Effects Puzzle Sheet

1 E L E L F I F I I F I F L E L E	**2** STEP PETS PETS	**3** **IT TI**
4 JUST*144*ICE	**5** **PICT RES**	**6** **FAIRY WOLF DUCKLING**
7 CUT CUT CUT	**8** **REVIRDTAES**	**9** YOUR1111LIFE
10 MONA LISA 123	**11** **PINN**A**CLES**	**12** **DAY DAY DAY** DAY

13
 	
**kcolc
kcolc**
	14
	
	wafibit
		15 Twink
		           Twink
		           Twink
		           Twink

Visual Effects Worksheet

(1) _____

(2) _____

(3) _____

(4) _____

(5) _____

(6) _____

(7) _____

(8) _____

(9) _____

(10) _____

(11) _____

(12) _____

(13) _____

(14) _____

(15) _____

About the Author

Lorraine L. Ukens is the owner of Team-ing with Success, an organization specializing in team building and leadership development. Her wide range of business experience, spanning more than twenty years, is applied in designing, facilitating, and evaluating programs in a variety of training areas.

In 1993, Lorraine developed a comprehensive three-phase training program, also called **TEAM-ING WITH SUCCESS,**™ which was designed to help build and maintain high-performing teams. Since then, additional games and activities have been developed that use hands-on learning experiences to promote constructive group dynamics.

Lorraine received her M.S. degree in human resource development from Towson State University in Maryland. A writer and consultant, she is an active member of the American Society for Training and Development.

Printed in the United Kingdom
by Lightning Source UK Ltd.
131811UK00001B/15-20/A

9 780787 903558